Buddha's

Six Classic Buddhist Teachings in Modern Verse

Tai Sheridan, Ph.D.

Buddha's Golden Light

Six Classic Buddhist Teachings in Modern Verse

ISBN-13: 978-1461165804
ISBN-10: 1461165806

Website: www.taisheridan.com
Email: tai@taisheridan.com

Also by Tai Sheridan
www.taisheridan.com

Buddha in Blue Jeans Contemplative Series

Buddha in Blue Jeans: An Extremely Short Zen Guide to Being Buddha

Relax...You're Going to Die

Secrets of True Happiness

Zen Prayers for Repairing Your Life

Buddhist Classics in Modern Verse

Celestial Music: Sutras of Emptiness /
The Lotus / Diamond / Heart-Wisdom / Loving Kindness Sutras

The Bare Bones Dhammapada: Big Mind Big Love / Buddha's Essential Teachings

The Buddhacarita: A Modern Sequel / The Poetic Saga of Buddha's Life From Birth to Enlightenment

The Zen Wheel of Life Mantra: A Song of Luminous Wisdom and Love / Based on the Bhavacakra - The Wheel of Life Mandala

Zen Classics in Modern Verse

The Light of the Ancient Buddhas: Ballads of Emptiness and Awakening / Based on Keizan's Transmission of the Light

Rice Eyes: Enlightenment in Dogen's Kitchen / A poetic

version of Dogen's Tenzo Kyokun on enlightened living and practice

Snow Falling in Moonlight: Odes in Praise of Dogen's Shobogenzo / Twelve Poems based on Dogen's Shobogenzo:The Treasury of the True Dharma Eye

Warm Zen Practice: A Poetic Version of Dogen's Bendowa Whole Hearted Way

Collections and Other Works

Buddha's Golden Light: Six Classic Buddhist Teachings in Modern Verse

Patanjali: Yoga Sutras in Lingo: The Liberation Spirit in Modern Metaphors

Table of Contents

Dedication

To the Great Mystery
of Living and Dying

Not all of us can do great things.
But we can do small things with great love.

- Mother Teresa

Introduction

Buddhism teaches you how to be a Buddha. In modern terms - you are big body, big heart, and big mind. The ancient wisdom in this book can help you recognize your authentic life outside of the ego's need for identity, security, and affirmation. It can support your honest evaluation of the aggressions and passions that interfere with inner peace. Most importantly, it can guide you toward the light body of Buddha, the dharmakaya.

Buddha's Golden Light compiles six of my previously published dharma books based on texts written from between the first through fourteenth centuries. Although the world has changed, the roots of human suffering remain the same, which makes these ancient teachings relevant, universal, and timeless.

I have re-visioned these classics to make Buddhist and Zen wisdom more accessible. Each work has been transformed into poetry which uses modern words and images. I have written brief introductions, thus allowing the reader to quickly understand the context of the works without having to absorb extensive historical, religious, and contextual information. This is also in keeping with my wish to evoke immediate experience and personal insight as the basis of true understanding.

The texts in this book are wide ranging and cover the essential spiritual teachings of Buddhism. The Lotus, Diamond, Heart, and Loving Kindness Sutras contain the essential teachings of Buddha. The Wheel of Life Mantra presents core Buddhist cosmology and philosophy. Keizan's esoteric Transmission of the Light is a mythic journey into enlightenment and the destruction of egoistic views. Dogen's seminal Zen writings include selections from Shobogenzo (Treasury of the True Dharma Eye), plus the complete versions of Bendowa (Whole Hearted Way) and Tenzo Kyokun (Instructions to the Cook). All of these works encourage awakening your big body, heart, and mind and bringing benefit to the world.

I am grateful to the men and women who have kept the Buddhist flame of spiritual inquiry burning brightly down through the centuries. I hope their wisdom will lead all beings deeper into the mountains of spiritual ease and delight.

- Tai Sheridan, Kentfield, 2011

Classic Buddhist and Zen Texts

Celestial Music
Sutras of Emptiness

Introduction to the Sutras

The Buddhist sutras present a path of enlightened living based on curiosity, good will, wisdom, and compassion. They offer the reader a journey through the mountains and valleys of human experience: living and dying, love and loss, anguish and peace.

Each sutra is unique: The Lotus Sutra represents the Bodhisattva path and is a lengthy compilation of parables in an archaic style. The Diamond Sutra is a short, but dense, treatise on non-dual dialectics, which illuminate the ground of Being. The Heart Wisdom Sutra expresses the balance of form and emptiness, and the Loving Kindness Sutra models a compassionate life.

I made significant changes to the English translation of the sutras. The ancient monks and nuns were steeped in altruistic spiritual attitudes, whereas most contemporary readers are unfamiliar with the life of vow. I have condensed, re-structured, and amplified the texts with an eye to modernizing them and to adding a universal appeal. In order to clarify and invoke the spiritual intentions of the sutras, I begin each one with a set spiritual intention.

The preludes to each Sutra, "Beating the Celestial Drum", are an old Zen device, a challenge to the reader that hints of meanings in the writing that follows. I hope these contemporary Sutra versions invite wonder, loving kindness, and peace.

The Lotus Sutra
The Bodhisattva Path

Introduction

The Lotus Sutra calls itself "the King of Sutras". This Sutra is the foundation of the Bodhisattva ideal that encourages spiritual awakening for the benefit of all beings. It contains parables that illuminate dharma teachings, practices, realization, and the transmission of truth.

The Lotus Sutra is an exploration of attitudes which create suffering, and it awakens the path of healing and transformation. It states that if someone truly hears one word or verse of the sutra then cosmic light will become their own body and they will become a Buddha.

The Buddhist concept of "no-self" is central to the Lotus Sutras, an idea that easily confuses people. "No-self" is a non-dualistic viewpoint in which there is no such thing as "a person" existing apart from the myriad phenomena of the universe. Buddha emphasizes this reality by insisting that even the concept of enlightenment is an illusion, for there is no "self" that can be enlightened. In other words, awakening is not something one attains, but is the dropping away of all conceptualizations of identity.

The challenge in transforming the book length Lotus Sutra into a brief poem and chant was to preserve the wisdom while eliminating redundancies, esoteric knowledge, archaic references, and the stylized writing of the original. I hope the reader discovers the beauty and majesty of the Lotus Sutra of the Wonderful Law in this modern version.

Beating the Celestial

The Lotus Sutra is the King of Sutras, the celestial drum parting heavens and a thunderous reality splitting the earth asunder. Your house is burning down! The path up the mountain of selflessness is steep. You will stumble while grasping at the illusion of a Self. Can you hear the call of the Lotus Sutra to awaken in the great commingling? Can you hear the cries of the world? Is your heart moved to embrace the totality of existence? When the lotus opens you will find happiness by nourishing the world. Once you hear the music, practice with your heart on fire. After realizing the way, wander the earth with gift bestowing hands.

The Lotus Sutra

In this brief life
May I treasure and liberate
All beings with wisdom and love

Thus have I heard of the Lotus Sutra

The Lotus Flower Sutra
of Wondrous Reality
Frees all from misery
Awakens joy and peace

Buddhas beat celestial drums
Shaking all things
A fragrant breeze
All things commingled

Dharma Rain
Subtle and mysterious
Free of twigs and leaves
The Seal of Reality

From the beginning
All things complete
With nothing to attain
Buddhas realize the Lotus Way

Thus have I heard
of Practicing the Way

Your house is burning down
Fueled by flames of desire
Listen with a unified mind
To Dharma beyond words

With a soft mind
And respectful heart
Pay homage to all Buddhas
Have faith in the Way

Delight in silent contemplation
Motionless in body and mind
Devote yourself to quiet places
Enjoy real nourishment

Stabilize in bodhisattva realms
Of action and intimacy
Harmonize with inter-being
Contemplate no self nature

With a pure loving heart
live the Undivided Way
Study Realize Teach
for the benefit of all beings

Thus have I heard
of Realizing the Way

Dharma rains pour on everything
Trees plants herbs flourishing
Sprinkled with sweet dew
Joyfully enter the Buddha-way

In mountains a bird song
Ear sound song without gap
All senses originally non-dual
Pure as lapis lazuli

People attach to shapes colors
The bodhisattva sees luminosity
The infinite boundless body
Revealed in the clay body

Hear the sound of spaciousness
The snap of buddhas fingers
echoes throughout the universe
Earth trembles with Realization

Practice endlessly
Realize instantaneously
All things impermanent
Without self nature

The earth splits open
Everything springs forth
Let the lamp blow out
Welcome infinite happiness

Be like the world-honored One
with wise and pure eyes
All nets of doubts gone
A heart peaceful as the sea

Thus have I heard
of Teaching the Way

Walk the Bodhisattva Path
With enthusiasm and courage
Awaken all Beings
from self centered activity

Buddha entrusts you with Reality
Wholeheartedly teach the Way
End the sorrows of
birth age disease death

All Buddhas past present future
Dispel darkness disperse gloom
Use infinite tactful means
Lead beings from attachments

Beating the Drum of Truth
Patiently reveal the essence
Teach according to each nature
Expect nothing in return

Be at ease and confident
Responsive and kind
Never anticipate
Never disparage

Be like a great cloud
Rise above the world
full of beneficial moisture
Pouring rain abundantly

Never weary of teaching
This King of Sutras
The Lotus of Wondrous Reality
Bringing gladness to all

The Diamond Sutra
Lightening in an Empty Sky

Introduction

The Diamond Sutra offers insight into the world of emptiness (shunyata) and the luminous transcendent Buddha body (dharmakaya). Diamond light symbolizes the universe as one's own being, often referred to in Zen as "the ten-thousand things" arising simultaneously and commingled in the present moment. Lightening is a Zen metaphor for Satori, the moment of awakening, which in reality is all moments of clear awareness.

The Sutra explores and expresses the ground of Being. All sutras strike a balance between the nuomenal and phenomenal worlds of emptiness and form, but it is the Diamond Sutra that most directly expresses the reality of emptiness.

The Diamond Sutra is brief, so my restructurings will be obvious to those familiar with it. I have changed the flow of the text to better integrate and present the meanings. I hope you enjoy the brilliance of the sutra as you might the morning star at dawn.

Beating the Celestial Drum

A flash of lightning in the midnight sky. Buddha roars yet you sleep through the night. The luminous diamond of reality penetrates to the farthest corners of the universe and yet is as close as your nose. It is the sound of your footsteps on moss and the breathing that supports your life. Do you still seek outside yourself as if there is an outside? How could there be anything to attain, you are already complete! Still your mind jumps about and passions drive you. If you would like to know Undivided Reality, sit down and be still, listen to the black crows of dawn. Give up trying and self-importance. Who is the doer and what is done? This diamond shines even in a cup made of clay. Are you ready to become truly human? Listen to the Diamond Sutra.

The Diamond Sutra

In this brief life
May I treasure and liberate all beings
With wisdom and love

Thus have I heard of the Diamond Body

A dewdrop a cloud a star
a flash of lightening in empty sky
without a fixed self anywhere
the Diamond Body includes all things

Thus have I heard of Calm Sitting

Countless truth seekers
sincere and fearless
clarify the Diamond Body
wishing benefit for all beings

Sitting upright and calm
with courage balance detachment
self centered intentions wane
the miracle of inter-being arises

Thus have I heard of Awakening

Grasping a cloud or star an impossibility
be one with spacious presence
Give freely - awaken!
Let go of identity – awaken!

Self centered foolishness
creates attachments disturbs harmony
See conditioned views as illusory
awaken the Diamond Body

With nothing to eliminate
Awakening not attaining a state
the Diamond Body without substance
actualizes true selflessness

Without attaining mind
subjects objects merge
no gap between things
everyone awakening simultaneously

Without attachment
all things brilliant unique
all things the luminous total dynamic
things and no-things instantaneous

All things arise in the present
beyond thinking and not thinking
beyond beginning end true false
beyond ignorance enlightenment self other

All things a confluence
of the world-cosmos
within spacious presence
each place sacred

Seeing things precisely
without self or attachment
the Diamond Body of No Body
beyond coming going birth death

Auspicious beyond name or concept
Present within shapes and colors
An incomprehensible subtle totality
The unconditioned unified world

Thus have I heard of Wise Living

Love awakens in an empty sky
patience tolerance grow
be awake in the Diamond Body
ordinary without special traits

Wise people treasure awakening
calm minds rest in the present totality
without gain or self inflated pride
live for the benefit of everything

Wise people renounce self centeredness
honor truth wherever spoken
clothe themselves in spacious presence
receive and manifest the great blessing

Wise people continually renew
the liberation of no liberation
intuitive wisdom recognizes no self
within Diamond Body no self to save

Wise people keep aspiration alive
All things clear light lacking substantiality
Without a promise of attainment
Diamond Body the original blessing

The Heart Wisdom Sutra
The Commingling of Things

Introduction

The Heart Wisdom Sutra is recited daily in Zen temples as the essential buddha-dharma reality in which there is no gap between self and other, and where all things arise simultaneously out of emptiness in the moment (co-dependent arising).

I have made significant changes to current versions of the sutra. The most famous phrase of the sutra, "form is emptiness and emptiness is form", expresses the dynamic relationship between phenomena and noumena, the commingling of things. I have changed this sacred verse to read "form and emptiness are one", a far easier concept to understand. I have changed the reference to the skandhas which reads "no eye, no ear, no nose, no body, no mind", to a more easily understood expression that "senses-sensing-sensed are one". I have used the meaning of Shariputra's name, "beautiful eyes", instead of his name itself.

The sutra ends in the transcendent and elegant line "Gate Gate Paragate Parasamgate Bodhi Svaha!": beyond beyond always going beyond yes! I hope this version of the sutra helps clarify the non-dual world of the Buddha-Dharma.

Beating the Celestial Drum

Do not be fooled by the earth and sky. Things will seduce you with their apparent solidity. Emptiness will seduce you with apparent luminosity. Things and no-things dance eternally in the present moment. If you cultivate great curiosity and manage not to be blinded by what you see, perhaps you can settle down and watch clouds drifting over green mountains. Trying to understand form and emptiness with your mind is like putting your pants on backwards. You can't figure it out! Still, you think there is a horizon that you can know. Go drown in the arising and co-mingling of existence! This is nothing other than sweeping the path and making tea. If you think it is something special you are truly lost. Just keep walking until you die.

Heart Wisdom Sutra

In this brief life may I treasure
And liberate all beings
With wisdom and love

With open and beautiful eyes
Invoke the compassionate wisdom of Avalokiteshvara
Clarify that all things have no fixed identity

Form and emptiness do not differ
Shape and spaciousness are one
Clarify everything as unique yet commingled

See clearly with a calm balanced view
Senses sensing sensed flowing undifferentiated
Clarify phenomena arising from unconditioned emptiness

With open and beautiful eyes
Everything unique interconnected
Dissipate the anguish of separation

Before emotions senses thoughts ideas
Before habits judgments views consciousness
Enter warm spaciousness the total dynamic

With open and beautiful eyes
Everything emanating from spaciousness
Enter the luminous realm of now

View things with complete acceptance
Old age death anguish knowing
Enter the infinite realm within beyond

Troubles and fears calmed
Trust rely on spacious wisdom
No special experience to attain

Throughout time people have awakened
By no longer viewing things as separate
Resting in spaciousness awakens complete being

The wisdom of spaciousness is the truthful
Incomparable mysterious light of existence
Each moment continuously going beyond the known

Gate Gate Paragate Parasamgate Bodhi Svaha

The Loving Kindness Sutra
Arms Open Wide

Introduction

The Loving Kindness Sutra is a blueprint for living a kind and wholesome life. The Sutra is founded on the wish for all beings to be happy, and describes the spiritual terrain of non-harming. For the meditation student, it is a confirmation of things seen and heard with a pure heart and clear mind.

I have changed some time honored phrases in the sutra, such as "a mother protects her only child", to "a parent protects". Although I appreciate the original phrase, I think that all care takers must be included as providers of true nurturing. I also changed the significant yet esoteric statement about wishing love toward "all beings in low, middle, and high realms of existence" by openly mentioning people of all races, colors, creeds, and capacities. I prefer specifics in this case rather than generalizations, for we must continually remind ourselves that prejudice is at the heart of pandemic disease, warfare, and threats to the earth's ecology.

Even though the sentiments of the sutra are easy to understand, it takes a lifetime to actualize Big Love in ourselves and our families, communities, work places, nations, and world. May all beings indeed be happy!

Beating the Celestial Drum

Everybody preaches love but who dares examine their own shadow? Ill will is hard to root out. And what of your grief and the unloved places that call out to you on a lonely night? When you go to bed full, how do you think about those who are hungry! When you go to bed hungry, how do you think about those who are full! When the playing field is leveled we are all brothers and sisters in a rocky boat. Let's row in cadence. Better yet, let us embrace and whisper what we already know. Love is all there is, love is all there is, love is all there is...

Loving Kindness Sutra

In this brief life
May I treasure and liberate
All beings with wisdom and kindness

May I live
kindly toward all
content and competent
honest with integrity
gentle and humble
speaking directly and truthfully
willing to learn

May I treasure
living simply without overextending
neither denying the senses nor overindulging
respecting all without self inflation
nourishing and supporting my life

May I not act in ways wise people might question

May all beings be happy
all genders races creeds
all bodies personalities roles
all capacities incapacities
all known unknown
all past present future beings

May all beings be happy
May I not deceive nor despise anyone
May I maintain good will and wish no harm

Like a parent protecting children
I open my boundless heart to all
Releasing all ill will
Never betraying loving kindness

May I practice mindful kindness in all activities
May love here-now be my spiritual foundation

With an open mind I am whole
With senses in balance I am healthy
With oneness I am peaceful
With an alert spacious mind I am free

The Light of the Ancient Buddhas
Ballads of Emptiness and Awakening

based on Keizan's Transmission of the Light

Introduction

Keizan's thirteenth century Denkoroku:The Transmission of the Lamp, is essentially a sophisticated Zen fairytale about enlightenment and shunyata, the empty ground of Being. Keizan uses archetypal myths, legends, and dreams to describe the luminous and awakened Zen mind. I transformed eighteen of his fifty-three stories into lyrical renaissance poetry, a form of story telling verse that mirrors the mythic quality of the original.

Although the ballad form is usually associated with the chivalrous and romantic tradition of Renaissance Europe, the spiritual subject matter of this book is clearly neither romantic nor chivalrous, but is instead a deep expression and inquiry into the essence of existence-Being.

One challenge in writing this work was to express the essence of Keizan's stories while using the highly structured rhyming pattern of the Ballad, ababbcbC, where cbC is a concluding envoi with C both rhyming and repeating in all four Stanzas. I began each of the Ballads with a non-traditional four line stanza that introduces the main character and provides a structural framework for the work as a whole. The main challenge was to rhyme without succumbing to triteness, erudition, or stultification.

I hope these mythic ballads shed light on the wisdom of the early Buddhist masters and serve as an inspiration for those inquiring into their own Buddha Nature and Universal Self.

The Ballad of Shakyamuni the Beggar

Welcome seeker of kind wisdom
I am Shakyamuni the Beggar
with warm hands transmitting light
teaching emptiness forthright

At dawn peacefully contemplating
the brightest morning star
a profound Reality arose most flowing
within mind's deepest reservoirs
no-self a swirling cosmic samovar
mental formations empty nature shown
as the dharma ocean essence without par
may all selfish ways be atoned

In silently witnessing
things just as they are
dharma wheel of emptiness turning
beyond infinite diamond stars
now needing just one bowl insofar
as anguish at last renounced disowned
the light body transcends near far
may all selfish ways be atoned

I bequeath you wise understanding
your enlightenment my noble memoir
awaken the path of not-knowing
with Manjusri's diamond scimitar
slicing non-dual ignorance apart
the moon light a birthstone

true mind no longer marred
may all selfish ways be atoned

Transmitting the dharma flower
marrow skin flesh bone
the eightfold path for abiders
may all selfish ways be atoned

The Ballad of Kashyapa the Drinker of Light

Welcome seeker of kind wisdom
I am Kashyapa the Drinker of Light
with warm hands transmitting light
teaching emptiness forthright

Buddha raised a flower imbuing
me with light a brilliant meteor
at last true nature according
I healed afflictions I deplore
and to precepts fully swore
thus bowing to dharma most revered
nowhere an I to enlighten evermore
may the light in your life appear

From master to master this flower raising
a dharma raft to other shore
awakening mind transcending
attachments repulsions no more
luminous darkness comes to fore
intellectual concepts veer
for light is inexplicable as lore
may the light in your life appear

Please pick up self studying
yet do not ten thousand things ignore
put to rest intellectualizing
turn the light within as you explore
that nothing remains solid at core
all Buddhas arise with you here
unlike views tightly held before

may the light in your life appear

Awakening wisdom of no shore
is following Buddhas path sans fear
your mind gives birth to our founder
may the light in your life appear

The Ballad of Ananda the Joyful

Welcome seeker of kind wisdom
I am Ananda the Joyful
with warm hands transmitting light
teaching emptiness forthright

Blessed with brilliant knowing
for years Buddha's attendant resolute
with a joyful presence bestowing
while teaching dharma roots
greed hate delusions transmute
the truth dharma sweetly imparts
investigate no-thing absolute
may bliss awaken within your heart

Studying concepts hindering
emptiness has no signs or attributes
mind tends toward meandering
focusing on breath most astute
for practicing out of view and mute
examine where conditioning starts
then awaken with nothing to refute
may bliss awaken within your heart

If you aspire to awakening
examine the useless pursuit
of success as if a noble bearing
for the uncreated there is no substitute
may gain and loss uproot
before this life departs

hear echo and response of lute
may bliss awaken within your heart

When truth arises you will never be destitute
for from no existing thing are you apart
mountains rivers your true nature constitute
may bliss awaken within your heart

The Ballad of Shanavasa the Cloth Wearer

Welcome seeker of kind wisdom
I am Shanavasa of Natural Clothing
with warm hands transmitting light
teaching emptiness forthright

Formed six years in womb most nurturing
my birth Buddha with vision did foretell
a sorcerer's apprentice with facility absorbing
magical formulas and arcane spells
as a fire dragon human darkness I dispelled
now wearing natural cloth in heat rain
after Ananda transmitted me dharma well
may you not waste your life in vain

Uncreated essence the uplifting
totality each Buddha's life retells
the light within most astounding
this hidden fact not known well
how form emptiness within it dwell
nothing produced nor producer of name
transcend mountain rivers forest dell
may you not waste your life in vain

Appearances deceive in arising
materialistic sight must be repelled
one eye alone transcends categorizing
the uncreated the sinews of your body shell
examine thoroughly desires that compel
as all lineage Buddhas explain
then go where anguish hath befell

may you not waste your life in vain

With wonder ring the dragon bell
deliver beings from six realms of pain
with Buddha's seal their anguish quell
may you not waste your life in vain

The Ballad of Upagupta the Demon Slayer

Welcome seeker of kind wisdom
I am Upagupta the demon slayer
with warm hands transmitting light
teaching emptiness forthright

With Shanavasa I sat abiding
anguish of desire curtailed
then the devil attacked berating
my dignity and viciousness impaled
my noble dharma parry subtly prevailed
around him a compassion garland I aligned
made of snake and dog corpse baled
may you liberate body and mind

The devil practiced contemplating
prostrating and repenting in minute detail
taking refuges absolving
lusty passions until derailed
a mountain of repose the devil scaled
attachments left behind
as well the dusty world's travails
may you liberate body and mind

Practice going beyond seeking
stopping or attaining sure to fail
with sacred and profane abating
no inside or outside avails
just once Buddha nature must you unveil
mind a mirror an autumn moon divined
impartially reflecting pebble stone shale

may you liberate body and mind

Zen teachers by existence fail
yet no traces ever left behind
lightening in an empty sky the holy grail
may you liberate body and mind

The Ballad of Dhrtaka the Great Mountain

Welcome seeker of kind wisdom
I am Dhrtaka the Great Mountain
with warm hands transmitting light
teaching emptiness forthright

Before birth my father lay dreaming
of golden suns and heavenly fire
and rivers in four directions flowing
a jewel adorned mountain spire
his vision my selfless self entire
when all forms were completely shed
my personal self died in reality's fire
may liberation to all be spread

Upagupta taught self death transcending
yet no person nor world exists to expire
true mind neither coming nor going
not a thing any effort can acquire
no book can replace heaven's gyre
open your treasure house instead
deep within existing enquire
may liberation to all be spread

Until you attain complete awakening
all Buddhas toward you carry ire
what demon made you go seeking
speaking of truth contemptuously dire
keeping silent still phenomenal mire
smash the universe until dead
with courage invite your funeral pyre

may liberation to all be spread

Buddha's liberating wisdom afire
in emptiness the pearl of light well bred
awakening reality no self transpires
may liberation to all be spread

The Ballad of Micchaka the Sorcerer

Welcome seeker of kind wisdom
I am Micchaka the Sorcerer
with warm hands transmitting light
teaching emptiness forthright

Six eons I slaved sorcery absorbing
with one thousand sorcerers cohorts stalwart
then I demanded pure avowing
stating black arts the dharma pervert
I must the true essence assert
all sorcerers avowed at my behest
to in the dharma our minds exert
may the uncreated rest within your breast

My decadent path most self-willing
true insight my arrogance did subvert
believing as a nihilist unrepenting
my forlorn spirit unable to convert
drunk on ignorance a spiritual braggart
thinking goals the guiding lights on the quest
with blind desires I strove for comfort
may the uncreated rest within your breast

Truth like ocean waves arising
the surface undulations merely overt
deep within movement nowhere flowing
the apparent and the real must invert
death in awakening neither stasis nor inert
living dying the matter to address
mirror mind the samadhi most alert

may the uncreated rest within your breast

All natural beings exist in concert
each moment's arising wondrously blessed
the diamond light nothing covert
may the uncreated rest within your breast

The Ballad of Vasumitra the Vessel

Welcome seeker of kind wisdom
I am Vasumitra the Vessel
with warm hands transmitting light
teaching emptiness forthright

In front of me a vessel filling
emptying transforming without end
Micchaka asked if in the way according
to whom it belonged to see if I'ld defend
a subject object gap that rends
the whole half rather than abides
in the uncreated which Buddha's tend
may the invisible become clarified

Clean clothes my style wearing
I bear a wine vessel others reprehend
my crazed whistling appears bastardizing
a hidden ancestry hard to comprehend
yet golden clouds from above descend
as Buddha foretold with eyes unified
he knew where in India I'ld ascend
may the invisible become clarified

The vessel a symbol of my teaching
the uncreated leaves nothing to fend
each thing named in truth disappearing
each phenomenon upon all others depends
nobody existing people misapprehend
transmission of light no-thing implies
Buddha's path I sincerely commend

may the invisible become clarified

Sweet emptiness all words transcend
no conception can dharma codify
skin flesh bones marrow to apprehend
may the invisible become clarified

The Ballad of Buddhanandi the Eloquent

Welcome seeker of wisdom
I am Buddhanandi the Eloquent
with warm hands transmitting light
teaching emptiness forthright

I am gifted with eloquence higher
named after Gautama and tales allegorical
my teacher Vasumitra challenged my manner
as a sophist and dialectic adept with sharp accusal
by dismissing talk of meanings as untraditional
discussion does not carry doctrine he explained
even profundities as nature is reality aberrational
may you treasure silence with speech restrained

Vimalakirti's silence a partial truth transmitter
but still a rendering most abysmal
neither words nor silence dharma carriers
were you born blind without vision able
to see inherent essence in all things remarkable
selflessness confuses those untrained
that seek to define the sacred relational
may you treasure silence with speech restrained

Do not seek emptiness to make you holier
beyond Buddhism and Zen awaits the accessible
to a dharma outside of coming or going demure
nobody is born or dies in this profound epistle
what you call body and dreams nonessential
master Dongshan in enlightenment exclaimed
I am not It and It is I as reality transcendental

may you treasure silence with speech restrained

All walls constructed most artificial
you must penetrate where no traces remain
everywhere is free and accessible
may you treasure silence with speech restrained

The Ballad of Punyamitra the Speechless

Welcome seeker of wisdom
I am Punyamitra the Speechless
with warm hands transmitting light
teaching emptiness forthright

My teacher Buddhanandi was kindlier
than most telling me I was his kin and in-law
closer to him than my parents altogether
for acting in accord with things awakens awe
this is Buddha's most profound universal law
your light brighter than a thousand suns lit
detaching from your parents a path most raw
may you enter gently the true family I transmit

Seeing white light above my house an indicator
Buddhanandi within a saint foresaw
confirmed because speaking I could not aver
so he proclaimed me a true vessel without flaw
and thus I was the successor he oversaw
already fifty years old I must admit
before the supreme path I saw
may you enter gently the true family I transmit

Your parents are not your kin nor progenitors
and Buddha is not your path to trod
this mystery of the source only you author
eyes ears depend not upon others or demigods
people and Buddhas as they are without facade
your own mind a jewel of dharma most benefit
neither sun nor moon as your mind broad

may you enter gently the true family I transmit

Zen transmits pointing beyond written law
like a mouth hanging in space close-knit
your mind your only kin and spiritual maw
may you enter gently the true family I transmit

The Ballad of Parshva the Never Sleeping

Welcome seeker of wisdom
I am Parshva the Never Sleeping
with warm hands transmitting light
teaching emptiness forthright

While attending Punyamitra the wisest
never sleeping while studying scriptures overall
in three years penetrating the uncreated rarest
the universal scriptures which had enthralled
noumena and phenomena both pitfalls
forget fatigue and study the aggregate heap
as within each moment all forms call
may you diligently neither reject nor keep

The eve before my birth my father closest
a white elephant in his dream recalled
with lustrous jewel that shone the amplest
on tiles pebbles trees fences beings all
I beg you to this jeweled light set your resolve
for though you see appearances you are asleep
yet beware conceit when grace befalls
may you diligently neither reject nor keep

Sixty years was I in womb then forest
so eighty when upon Punyamitra I called
most said I was to old but this doubt a catalyst
to recite the precepts and shave my head bald
not sleeping during day or nightfall
becoming a vessel into which light could seep
every day is a good day the essence to recall

may you diligently neither reject nor keep

Born wherever you stand in realms all
unto death each moment must you leap
let light emanate from feet hands eyeballs
may you diligently neither reject nor keep

The Ballad of Punyayashas the Golden Ground

Welcome seeker of wisdom
I am Punyayashas the Golden Ground
with warm hands transmitting light
teaching emptiness forthright

My teacher Parshva wanting to stay abreast
of my alertness asked with subtle tact
where do I come from could I attest
I replied mind is not in movement nor rest
he asked if I was uncertain as a deeper test
I replied Buddhas the same truth did fathom
then he said you are not the Buddhas yet
may you illuminate the inner golden dynamism

While sitting under a tree my teacher loftiest
right hand pointing did not hold back
saying if it turns golden we will be blest
by a sage with intuitive and illumined knack
who will bring the surname Gautama back
and Buddhist precepts transmitted for altruism
though of the transcendental you must lose track
may you illuminate the inner golden dynamism

For three weeks with mind focused sharpest
I sat until forgetting my own mind and back
and thus profoundly awakened sweetest
liberation from Buddhists while the aphrodisiac
of enlightenment no longer a setback
nor traces of Way seeking elitism
or separating inside outside white black

may you illuminate the inner golden dynamism

All concepts will take you well off track
purity and emptiness can make you numb
Zen and Buddhas themselves subtle drawbacks
may you illuminate the inner golden dynamism

The Ballad of Ashvaghosha Excellent in Virtue

Welcome seeker of wisdom
I am Ashvaghosha the Excellent in Virtue
with warm hands transmitting light
teaching emptiness forthright

I asked Punyayashas about truth holier
'that which does not know' his first portent
yet if not knowing the wisdom of ancestors
how can cognition or knowing be circumvent
he then cut me asunder with sharp comment
and my foolishness I did at last belie
virtue arising from the source a consequence
may the treasure of the dharma eye clarify

All Zen masters study Buddha with ardor
not through signs or sounds does it orient
the thirty-two marks not the true ancestor
eighty kinds of refinement still not an answer
sometimes eight arms three heads bearing antlers
or immersed in misery Buddha fully realized
liberate many once an awakened teacher
may the treasure of the dharma eye clarify

In infinite darkness no knowledge higher
Nowhere to discriminate or augment
it can't be found in shape or timbre
yet it follows you through eon's events
ocean waves rising falling the cosmic foment
this your original face yet don't go awry
thinking it the face of Buddha this moment

may the treasure of the dharma eye clarify

Teaching transforms folks to sages shrewder
as birth and death not feared now an ally
'not knowing' the home of the true abider
may the treasure of the dharma eye clarify

The Ballad of Kapimala the Demon

Welcome seeker of wisdom
I am Kapimala the Demon
with warm hands transmitting light
teaching emptiness forthright

When Ashvaghosha the dharma enunciator
said mountains rivers earth are Its abode
that powers and insights which arise superior
from emptiness manifest Buddha's robes
into the eightfold path I made subtle inroads
where walls and shards illumine It well hence
seeing and hearing have no limit imposed
may alertness to arisings unknown commence

As a demon I evoked my hateful power
storm winds rain out of black sky billowed
from within a flat rounded cloud lenticular
a gigantic golden dragon fire bellowed
scorching Ashvaghosha's equanimous mode
yet still he kept upon his seat bearing offense
and my tricks like rusting iron did corrode
may alertness to arisings unknown commence

I produced oceans as a trance attainer
but Ashvaghosha asked if this be followed
by oceans of essential nature worthier
out of which all realities have flowed
not a thing from outside is hallowed
once appearances no long seeming dense
no duality does original nature bestow

may alertness to arisings unknown commence

An old zen master body bent and bowed
said become a reflecting mirror whence
mind awakens all things with no abode
may alertness to arisings unknown commence

The Ballad of Nagarjuna the Supreme Dragon

Welcome seeker of wisdom
I am Nagarjuna the Supreme Dragon
with warm hands transmitting light
teaching emptiness forthright

I meditated in a stone cave deepest
whereupon a python encircled me abruptly
twas a monk transfigured for being an alchemist
mistakenly seeking truth sans camaraderie
upon meeting he awoke from one sided reverie
Kapimala asked of dharma gem proverbial
if it was form or formless in profundity
may you realize the wish fulfilling jewel

No special place exists for reality to manifest
do not cling to ancient views stubbornly
or vainly put yourself ahead of the rest
the masters abided in solitude absorbingly
only to ripen after enlightenment's clarity
you will become a spoiled seed deplorable
if training without teacher or assembly
may you realize the wish fulfilling jewel

I acquired super normal powers focused
and mastered paths with prodigious ability
upon seeing scripture titles I was blessed
yet still I was lost in paradox and ambiguity
for these outside paths were in aberrancy
only in Kapimala's discipleship classical
was the vast clear eye opened astutely

may you realize the wish fulfilling jewel

Master Xuansha stated most assuredly
the universe is a single bright jewel accessible
renunciate worldly ties with alacrity
may you realize the wish fulfilling jewel

The Ballad of Kanadeva the Ritualist

Welcome seeker of wisdom
I am Kanadeva the Ritualist
with warm hands transmitting light
teaching emptiness forthright

I was a famous spiritual philosopher
performing rituals throughout the nation
a learned intellectual and debater
the merit of good deeds my acclamation
until Nagarjuna confronted conceit so brazen
asking if enlightened nature I did revere
thus arrogance I completely abandoned
may you accord with heart mind sincere

After visiting my blessed dharma teacher
I cultivated Buddha's intimate doctrine
yet Nagarjuna tested me as a reminder
a water bowl with needle he did offer
I floated the needle on top with rapture
thus penetrating non-duality without fear
in all directions Buddha's offered flower
may you accord with heart mind sincere

We shared the teaching seat together
as did Kashyapa after his induction
like snow in a silver bowl the mind's interior
Nagarjuna became the full moon with acumen
transmitting the formless beyond secular
not wide narrow large small without limitation
the dharma of wide-open clarity consider

may you accord with heart and mind sincere

Raising eyebrows is mixing with abandon
teacher and student simultaneously disappear
like squash vine's entwining configuration
may you accord with heart mind since

The Ballad of Rahulata the Eye of the Way

Welcome seeker of wisdom
I am Rahulata the Eye of the Way
with warm hands transmitting light
teaching emptiness forthright

A garden fungus a wild treat
a rich man and son most fond of eating
by magic the mushroom sprouted complete
though picked clean from tree's twinning
a monk in believer's alms receiving
caused this when emptiness he couldn't behold
upon which hearing Rahulata's awakening
may you give up your body for dharma gold

Of Rahulata Buddha dreamed complete
a thousand years before his birthing
of refined discernment he wouldst entreat
of his utmost rejection of water exploiting
based on enlightened conscience abhorring
all defilements and desecrations one beholds
give gratitude to parents for miraculous being
may you give up your body for dharma gold

Without a clear eye just a shameless thief
receive alms of grace in daily living
not beholden by basest conceits
observe as a beginner the way revealing
don't wait 'til light from eyes are waning
truth rarer than Udumbara a thousand fold
pay back the faithful by whole self dying

may you give up your body for dharma gold

Nothing has ever existed blocking
shedding body and mind before you're old
no one to stop no stopping no self doing
may you give up your body for dharma gold

The Ballad of Sanghanandi the Stabilized

Welcome seeker of wisdom
I am Sanghanandi the Stabilized
with warm hands transmitting light
teaching emptiness forthright

At birth I could speak truth firsthand
praising dharma giving reality due
at seven tiring of pleasures grand
with a monk at home I could construe
light as essential dharma to imbue
I awoke at hearing Rahulata's overture
that he bid his apparent self adieu
may the stable selfless self be yours

One eve a heavenly light fanned
upon an even road of golden hue
I ambled to a cliff yonder and
found peace in a cave without ado
then in twenty-one days arose renewed
Rahulata visited as a provocateur
asking if mind and body were askew
may the stable selfless self be yours

Letting go of body and mind disbands
the self centered nature misconstrued
Buddha's dharma an open hand
where nothing called self accrues
teachers students meet in empty milieu
the physical elements never endure
you are the teacher the teacher you

may the stable selfless self be yours

A shame when resolve is bland
clarify transmitted light pure
throughout body mind sky sand
may the stable selfless self be yours

The Zen Wheel of Life Mantra

A Song of Luminous Wisdom and Love

Introduction

The Bhavacakra is an ancient mandala that presents the most significant wisdom teachings of Buddhism. It is used to contemplate the causes and conditions of suffering, and as a guide to spiritual transformation on the path of non-dual wisdom, loving kindness, compassion, and equanimity.

I have written the The Wheel of Life Mantra as a poetic expression of the Bhavacakra. The poem opens by introducing spaciousness as the ground of being, the womb of existence within which the wheel turns. This is symbolized in the Tibetan tradition by Yama, the Lord of Death, and represents the infinite realms of time, space, impermanence and the unconditioned nature of being.

The Wheel is constructed of four concentric circles around a hub, each circle representing different areas of human experience and awareness. Beginning with the innermost circle and moving outward, they represent the dimensions of anguish, consequences, psychological experience, and the workings of consciousness. The wheel itself is an expression of the essential Buddhist teachings of no-self (nothing exists as a separate entity), impermanence (everything changes), and co-dependent origination (all phenomena arise simultaneously in reality in the present moment).

The Wheel is usually associated with he Tibetan school of Buddhism. The essential wisdom of the mandala is also deeply embedded within Zen writings, lectures, poetry, and art. The Wheel, like all Buddhist teachings, is an encouragement to find the way to peace, love, and light.

May all beings be happy!

The Zen Wheel of Life Mantra

The Zen Wheel of Life Mantra
Buddha's generous song
of Luminous Wisdom and Love

The Zen Wheel
turns on the axis
of emptiness

Its myriad spokes
seamless moments
of infinite time

Its garments
luminous dark
spaciousness

Whole heartedly enter
the mysterious way
of the unconditioned

The wheel
contains the whole
of myriad existences

Delicately held
by jaws of death
King of Impermanence

Transform anguish
into warm presence
May you live beneficially

Pay close attention
to the great commingling
May you harm no more

Meet the obstacles
of six realms
May you transform your character

Refining your attention
each arising moment
is the whole of it

Travel the wheel
liberate all
from apparent isolation

The Zen Wheel of Life Mantra
Buddha's generous song
of Luminous Wisdom and Love

The Circle of Anguish

I enter the circle
of bewilderment and anguish
the truth of unhappiness

I am the pig
groveling in lust
chasing mind filaments

I entitle myself
to desire myriad things
an illusion of true fulfillment

I am the snake
sidewinding hatred
bashing people and things

I entitle myself
to strike out at the world
an illusion of true fulfillment

I am the rooster
crowing self importance
a world unto myself

I entitle myself
to self centered living

an illusion of true fulfillment

Oh wise buddhas shine on me!
Oh loving bodhisattvas transform me!
Oh commingled mystery awaken me!

May my lust
transform into contentment
I am peace in life

May my enmity
transform into loving kindness
I embrace all life

May my selfishness
transform into sympathetic oneness
I am one with life

Now I awaken
the heartfelt desire
for the well being of all

May All Beings Be Happy
May All Beings Be One
May All Beings Be Free

The Circle of Consequences

I enter the circle
of consequences
my activity ripples the matrix

I have acted unwisely
harming myself and others
sorrow upon sorrow

In darkness I have descended
into anxiety depression worse
the maw of great unhappiness

I drown
dragging the world
down with me

I have yet to learn
kindness begets kindness
harm begets harm

Oh let me hear
the dharma rain
of non-harming

Oh let me hear
that each action
ripples the entire cosmos

Oh let me hear
that each step
spins the earth

I am the clear one
knowing my intentions
moving with tact

I am the responsive one
studying reactivity
walking with care

I am the beginning one
meeting the world anew
each dawning moment

As light and dark
compliment each other
like phases of the moon

May all of my
actions merge
in essential goodness

The path of consequences
wends through mountains rivers
a vast heart mind

May All Beings Be Happy
May All Beings Be One
May All Beings Be Free

The Circle of Six Realms

Invitation

I enter the circle
of six transmuting realms
each a mirror of my being

Not only one self
many manifestations
of difficulty and grace

The three realms above
seemingly dwell in light
I forget things come and go

The three realms below
seemingly dwell in darkness
I forget things come and go

The Human Realm

I enter the human realm
face arms legs breath
stunning miracle of life

I am needs longings
I am friends family work
I am the potential human

I am dignity because I was born
I am dignity because I live
I am dignity because I die

May I live humbly
in the human family
treasuring the miracle of life

The Hungry Ghost Realm

I enter the hungry ghost realm
decrepit malnourished starving
unable to find true nourishment

I am the lonely one
I am the unloved child
I am the unwitnessed being

I am full because I am
I am full because I give
I am full because I love

May I live fulfilled
easy to please and delight
a smile in each exchange

The Titan Realm

I enter the titan realm
so many graceful blessings
lost in pride and envy

I am jealous of blessed ones
denying ego's solid grip
falling from daily grace

I am whole already
I am unique already
I am awake already

May I delight in other's joy
unconcerned with fate
content with my lot

The Animal Realm

I enter the animal realm
raw instincts arising
grabbing pushing annihilating

Primitive naïve untrained
yet to hear the celestial drum
I justify the wily senses

I am the body at ease
I am the joy of emotion
I am ground and center

May I practice sincerely
resting in peaceful moments
allowing sensations to come and go

The Heavenly Realm

I enter the heavenly realm
awake blissful reposed
delighting in play of Mind

One thought of attachment
a world of suffering born
thinking this is it! opens hell's gate

All existence my Buddha Body
without a self Pure Mind
ordinary as grass in Spring

May I welcome commingling
remembering everything as Buddha
non attachment the way

The Hell Realm

I enter the hell realm
burning in delusional thought
on fire with my harmful ways

I suffer a living death
unhappy to my core
the doors of peace afar

I am the truth of suffering
I am the opportunity of learning
I am the seed of awakening

May I suffer consciously
heal and transform
on the luminous path

Blessing

The six realms
each light and shadow
infinite circles of being

In attachment weeds grow
in aversion leaves fall
may I let go continuously

Awake in the moment
witnessing experience
I study the gap of duality

May sight seen sound merge
may I walk daily
into the mist of not-knowing

May All Beings Be Happy
May All Beings Be One
May All Beings Be Free

The Circle of Arising Reality

Invitation

I enter the circle
of arising reality
things as they are

All points of the wheel
empty of self nature
mirroring the infinite whole

Twelve links
within and beyond
cause and effect

Four circles spinning
on the axis of emptiness
flowing through each other

The Blind Man

avijja – ignorance

I wander blind drunk
on this dusty road
tripping over myself

Disconnected from
true intimacy
in the world

My hunger
for love and meaning
leaves me anguished

Where will I find
there is more
to life

The Potter

samskaras - volitional action

I live from habits
old reactions drives
views I'm stuck on

Spinning like potter wheels
endlessly busy scattered
frustrated with the mess

From what clay
shall I make a cup
to drink from

From what stream
shall I sip
to fill my thirst

Monkey Climbs a Flowering Tree

vijnana - arising consciousness

From moment to moment
body heart mind
things not one not two

Monkey mind moving
swinging thoughts emotions
within just so moments

Arrow points
meeting in mid air
a thunderous awakening

Lotus petals open
now now now
unborn past future

Four People in a Boat

nama rupa - mind body

What I call body
is an open party
for everyone onboard

Not one part of me
beats grows moves
without all others

Why do I persist
in substantiating myself
over and again

Despite my wounds
and cryptic actors
the moon always full

House Windows Five Doors

shaddayatanas - senses

Gazing at red poppies
through windows
eyes poppies sight

In spring I breathe
the fragrant nectar
of sweet wisteria

Some people
call it insight
for me no name

Wax still remains
in my ears
sounds come from afar

A Couple Embraces

sparsha - contact

In this big place
let's embrace
hold hands walking

We've never parted
yet seemingly alone
between us a thread

Where am I
a drop of rain
or one moon

A flash of lightening
a clap of thunder
no second person

A Man With Arrow in Eye

upadana - grasping

Every day world
moving around
through me

My arrowed eyes
orbs of pleasure pain
endless cycling

Yet neutrality
unconcerned about
what's under skin

With calm breathing
I settle rest
in acceptance

A Woman Offers a Man a Drink

trishna - thirst

Some days I drink
her offered waters
other days not

My sweet tooth
insatiable madness
refined proclivities

Complete delusion
controlling life
tenacious self will

I've heard
of a middle road
gardens of peace

A Man Gathers Fruit

upadana - grasping

Grabbing ripe persimmons
overextending again
thinking all okay

Proud fool
stubborn convictions
Still seeking great heights

Round and round
wanting and resenting
reinforcing inner troops

A friend said
look within wake up
inside this mess

A Pregnant Woman

bhava - becoming

Within pear belly
mother child
not separate

No certainty
for me in birth
each moment wild

One two mixing
all born simultaneously
wonder upon wonder

Mysterious inter-being
takes up residence
in bones marrow

A Woman Gives Birth

jati - giving

A mysterious tunnel
woman birthing an infinite child
earth heaven gushing now

Life waters flow
with cosmic rain
all things family

Your mothers face
before she was born
see the whole dynamic

I am this
filling emptying
the spacious womb

A Corpse

jaramarana - decay and death

I am a corpse
on river banks
great spiritual death

Buddha awoke
the morning star
living dying treasure

Stars for eyes
mountains for feet
each breath beyond

Today a good day
beginner's mind
original blessingThe Blessing

Twelve stones
on a path to nowhere
walking with calm alertness

Honestly studying myself
courageously releasing myself
avoiding harming

May I die
the great death
and awaken Reality

From the beginning
I am Buddha
the authentic me

May All Beings Be Happy
May All Beings Be One
May All Beings Be Free

Dogen's Masterworks

Rice Eyes

Enlightenment in Dogen's Kitchen

Introduction

Handle Rice as if it is your own eyes – Dogen Paraphrase

Dogen lived from 1200 to 1253. He was the founder of the Soto lineage of Zen in Japan, a school of Zen now firmly rooted in America and the West. His seminal essay, Instructions to the Cook (Tenzo Kyokun), is an important treatise on living an aware and joyful life while engaged in daily activities.

'Rice Eyes' is a metaphor for the non-dual world, the essential Buddhist experience of oneness. Dogen uses the role of Tenzo, or head cook, to demonstrate how to live, work, and experience a joyful spiritual life that brings benefit to everyone. I have called the head cook the 'Chef de Cuisine' so that the poem addresses everyone, not just monastic Zen chefs.

I have transformed Dogen's essay from prose into poetry, and have created subdivisions by topic that clarify his writing. I have also replaced his thirteenth century idioms with contemporary language and images to make his ideas more easily understood.

Chef de Cuisine

welcome to dogen's kitchen
zen cooking down through time
cooking full attention everywhere
blood vein deriving from buddha
chefs de cuisine circles of light
steeping stillness attention letting go
cooking with buddha hands
being in charge tenzo chef de cuisine
appointed by life family friends food
nourishing everyone

chef de cuisine working devotedly
lovingly managing meals for hungry
cooking by vow calm clear connected
keeping spirit whole direct humble
throwing self into cooking
only possible failing not caring
awakening mind all tasks
wondrous variety differing needs occasions
one way cooking
helping all awakening

old great ones
cooking buddha's kitchen
guishan dongshan chefs de cuisine
kitchen working ordinary stirring pots
shop wash chop cook serve no big deal
your spirit the nourishment
dogen getting tips from old cooks
learning zen marrow
passing down rice eyes
any grub cooking most refined fare

Rice Eyes

chef de cuisine
working one whole day completely
checking cabinets fridge shelves
seeing what's in front of nose
rice vegetables condiments the works
dogen's cooking secret crystal clear
handling everything as own eyes
pot lid saucer spoon ladle
rice carrot lettuce beet radish
the whole universe - rice eyes!

touching food profound respect
gifts for royalty homeless all
touching kindly raw food cooked food
your own hands no other's
cooking between you food buddha
cooking today planning tomorrow flowing
planning with other cooks family friends
flavors seasonings dishes
how much just enough
tell all hide nothing

putting whole attention working
no lazing about doing it yourself
inquiring what situations demand
no knocking about absentmindedly
perfectionism ignores big picture
cooking oceans of virtue mountains of goodness
cooking harmoniously or nobody served
washing rice taking out sand
seeing rice seeing sand seeing sand seeing rice
fine meal naturally

Rolling Up Sleeves

old ones cooking nearby
cooking as form emptiness
washing sand picking rice
washing rice picking sand
using rice eyes
washing throwing out simultaneously
one eye tipping
the rice bucket
no dramatic personae
just washing cooking mind
going along sans fussing

rice sand fundamentals
rolling up sleeves
lost in cooking
wise ones settling down
working curious minds
own hands touching wasting nothing
keeping mind glued
all turning out well
paying attention being yourself
each rice grain mattering

re-using water no wasting
cleaning everything pouring rice
nobody peeking prodding hot pots
cleaning replacing pots ladles tools
high things on high places naturellement
low things on low places naturellement
gravity the root of grace
staying alert cleaning up
no thrashing mind about

Pot is Head

palms joining blessing food
singing to kitchen spirit
well cut gourmet discount wilted
no complaining regarding food
ridding comparisons
lots little good bad better worse
focusing mind seeing food
whole garden family
no room for whiners
incompetent cooking not

all day night just so moments
letting things come reside in mind
mind self being functioning whole works
mind universe cooking together now
before midnight getting ready for it
after midnight getting ready for it
soaking rice measuring water
standing at sink full presence
keeping eyes open
not losing one rice grain

seeing pot as head
seeing water as life blood
washing filling lighting cooking
rice soup salad heating all at once
bamboo baskets wooden bowls serving
seed shoots harvest rice wash cook serve
teaching zen cooking loving assistants
showing rice eyes shutting big mouth
chef de cuisine the kitchen pillar
heaven earth trembling

Build Temples From Greens

preparing mind the essence
rice not just a grain of rice
feelings besides the point
build great temples from greens!
chop wash clean expounding buddhadharma
tossing out likes dislikes greens really matters
no jumping for joy at special dishes
no moping over plain fare
beginner's mind not depending on quality
conforming to things not the way
devoting life spirit strengthening resolve
surpassing teacher's meticulousness refinement
applying life aspiration functioning for the way
way seeking mind the most important thing
plain soup from greens for a pittance
fine soup from greens for a pittance
no simple matter times have changed
scrupulousness total vitality passing muster
high aspiration sans arrogance
passing on rice eyes cooking way

uh oh oh no
horse mind running wild in fields
monkey mind swinging from trees
taking backward step stop look listen
life naturally one with work
simultaneously turning being turned
clarifying harmonizing absolute practical
correctly handling single green leaf
leaf manifesting buddha buddha manifesting leaf
free dynamism settling benefiting everything

Just Enough

eyes shut count all eating
do the math dharma numbers
one grain might be one grain
one grain might be one half grain
one grain might be two half grains
two half grains might be one grain
seeing surplus clearly
taking one away not enough
adding one too much
just enough the zen way

eating rice becoming guishan
adding a grain becoming cow
cow eating guishan guishan pasturing cow
counting again one two three
teaching according to capacity
using ingenuity practicing
seeing cow guishan one not two
temporarily cow guishan appearing separate
day to day remembering
one body one moment

money flowing
everyone figuring allocations
ancient sangha way
regarding all needs
no stepping on toes
remembering place
blessing rice serving rice
rice eyes cooking stability
don't waste time

Mushroom Men

preparing meals
buddhadharma par excellence
cooking way zen teaching
bowing thanking blessing food
sad people stuffing faces
old man lu drying mushrooms
crane white eyebrows sinew back
no hat bare feet hot sand sweating
mushroom man carrying load
quelle travaille fantastic!

old man of ayuwang
noodle soup chef de cuisine
walking forever searching mushrooms
never sloughing off cooking
nobody else souping
knowing practice knowing characters
buddha laughing roundly
short life hour always late
returning home returning home
mushroom way chef de cuisine

characters one two three four five
sitting standing lying down
all activities practice
nothing hidden world
truth cannot be grasped
moon in wave next wave too
two sided mushroom something nothing
ingenuity rice eyes grasping real zen
bottom of kettle beyond appearance
mushrooms always tasty

Oven Mouth

chef de cuisine practicing incomparable buddha way
mushroom men handing down
cooking way all working ways
meticulous care creating plenty
giving food clothing bedding medicine
shakyamuni died anointing chef de cuisine
eyebrow light gracing humans
serving sans fear not fearing serving
poverty enrichment middle way
unlimited mind unlimited fortune

good food bad food never grumbling
steady innards facing oven heat
respecting things as they is
old rice water original blessing
offering temple dates last dying act
sincere offerings buddha bond
small offerings big sincerity buddha bond
big offerings small sincerity not cooking way
human being practice
natural authentic sincere

choice ingredients not necessarily best soup
ordinary greens not necessarily worst soup
wholehearted handling the secret ingredient
pure mind pure heart no evaluation
delicacies plain tastes no distinctions
world as it is things as it is
cultivating aspiration cultivating rice eyes
a person's mouth an oven
heat melts everything together
whatever greens you have use well

Cooking Fool

foolish judging respectfulness worthlessness
long practice short practice neither wins
sans stability good bad reversing
differences abound so what
gifted not gifted stupid wise
just way seeking mind rice eyes
everybody treasured buddha child
forgiving mistakes wondrous dignity
going beyond right wrong
a fool a sage who can say

actualizing incomparable wisdom
blessings good fortune
one false step lost way
zen marrow total spirit infusion
noble chef de cuisine
foolish gabbing laziness busyness
not touching pot not thinking
rice eyes cooking the buddhist way
sans way seeking mind empty hands
no mountain goodness no ocean virtue

meeting teachers revealing cooking
aspiration awakening incomparable life
three attitudes the whole deal
benefiting others benefiting oneself
community working revitalizing character
going beyond teachers learning from lives
fool sees self as another
wise person sees others as self
sans true teacher feelings emotions rule
foolish people tossing out treasures

Three Minds

daigui awakening as chef de cuisine
dongshan awakening as chef de cuisine
realizing most important thing
no time more precious than now
child offering sand treasure
maintaining three minds
joyful magnanimous parental minds
grateful spirit joyful buoyancy
manifesting universal activity

born human miraculous amazing
no human no awakening no dharma drive
meal preparing vital important profound
cooking turning the wheel
community most precious
community sans pettiness
refined postures sans fabrication
lucky being human
lucky cooking rice eyes way
lucky serving three treasures

being human grateful joyous
so many births bad luck
heavenly realms divas pleasure attachment
hell realms self centered isolated angry sad
hungry ghosts love starved insatiable
animals beasts instincts ruling
asuras demons fighting jealousy reigns
nefarious bad luck no community practicing
limitations afflictions suffering burdens
no hands offering food

birth in world rejoicing yes!
using body freely offering food freely
honoring buddha dharma sangha
timeless universe marvelous opportunity
chef de cuisine merit never decaying
cooking at total capacity past present future
wholeheartedly in every moment every day
chef de cuisine cooking rice eyes way
connecting buddha dharma
joyful mind the attitude

parental mind loving children
loving three mind treasures
parental loving nourishing within difficulty
loving deep ocean high moon
parents forgetting selfish ways
protecting kids coral shade sun
living joyful mind second nature
handling water ice affectionately
everything parental caring
unconditional loving sans reward

magnanimous mind stable mountain
wide broad ocean views
no prejudice taking sides
an ounce not light
fifty pounds not heavy
spring can't carry you away
colors of fall sans heavy heart
seasons changing one whole time
balancing close broad perspectives
studying giving away magnanimous mind

fu awakening laughing out loud
guishan awakening blowing dead firewood
dongshan awakening three pounds flax
all cooking way seekers magnanimous
events circumstances the teachers
hearing voices expounding fundamentals
eyes wide open practicing living
pointing at moon pointing at plum blossoms
living true functioning living true self
rice eyes cooking

Snow Falling in Moonlight

Odes in Praise of Dogen's Shobogenzo

Introduction

In the snow a single twig of plum blossoms!

The whole universe is plum blossoms.

- Dogen

Dogen (1200-1253) is the father of Soto Zen. One of his spiritual legacies, The Shobogenzo (The Treasury of the True Dharma Eye), is composed of ninety-five essays on non-dual wisdom, luminous mind, loving kindness, and Zen practice. Dogen's essays express his insights into the Buddha Nature, or the Universal Self, a realm of awareness where there is no gap between self and other, doing and being, a plum blossom and the universe.

The odes presented here evolved from the central teaching of Dogen's essays and are structured and built upon his images. I based my selections on what I thought would be of interest and use to all Buddhists and to the public, not only to Zen students. I also chose pieces that would enchant and enlighten.

There is a legacy of Zen poetry that praises all manner of living things. I hope the Odes reveal the wonder and mystery of human life and open the mind of spiritual curiosity and inquiry.

In Praise of Dogen

you walked
in deep mountains
spring plum blossoms
the blessing

the vermillion petals
you loved well
grace the path
of western gardens

snow falling
in moonlight
the flame
of your vow

- Tai Sheridan

Ode To Moon

tsuki

i whisper praise
to lovely round moon
my own true body
vast endless space
moon in water
rising as whatever

moon not new not old
tonight's moon not yesterday's
you can't count how many
one two a zillion
give up comparisons
settle into now moon

i walk on earth
with mind-moon
full and complete
swallowing everything
mind is moon
moon is mind

subjects objects
meet in moon
moon is moon
living dying the moon
coming going the moon
day night the moon

swallowing the moon
is realizing myself
retching the moon
is going beyond
realizing myself
forever many moons

the cloud and moon
walking together
not starting stopping
beyond beginning ending
in quiet contemplation
a truly lovely moon

Ode to Time

uji

i whisper praise
to the fecund moment
snow falling in moonlight
mountain is time
pine is time
snow is time

once a child
building snowmen
now an old man
scribbling in snow
the child did not
become the man

a snow moment comes
a snow moment goes
it doesn't linger
complete as falling snow
complete as melting snow
only flowing snow

in the middle
of snowfield
i raise an eyebrow
winking at moon
smiling at
moon winking back

when eyebrows
freeze with frost
no winking at her
nor she winking back
winking eye light
a moment's play

wherever i find myself
the wondrous me
not past not future
i am snow
blue pine
time being

Ode to Space

koku

i whisper praise
to skin flesh bones marrow
body of infinite space
nostrils filling with it
space rests in palm
no gap in the fabric

let me play
in vast buoyancy
in gravity of nothing
words from an empty well
every thought space
space every thought

the wind bell
rings in the garden
blown from all directions
from head to toes
i am an open mouth
hanging in space

in the repose
of silent wall gazing
wall is mind
in snow fields
mind a withered pine
every shape sings space

using time well
taking charge of time
each moment space
in out breathing
the heart vein
open door to sky

small stones small
big stones big
no judgment here
infinite spacious mind
seeing only present
true dharma eye

Ode to Cedar Trees

hakujushi

i whisper praise
to cedar tree
many limbed buddha
awake in old garden
straw sandal joshu
a withered old cedar

special teas
won't spark cedar nature
i embrace space
truth seeking mind
learning from children
giving freely to elderly

life is tough
sometimes soup thin
often cold wins out
without profound sincerity
i chase things around
as if separate

when waking at dawn
i dress as cedar
now i am boss
coming going freely
not bound by in out
just being myself

majestic cedar tree
keeps going beyond
not grabbing water
not offending birds
cedar being cedar
is water and birds

cedar springing up buddha
sky falls down to earth
both now together
things common sacred
singing harmonious songs
beyond anything definable

Ode to Face Washing

senmen

i whisper praise
to face washing
bathing dust dirt
renewing total cleanliness
within without
body moon purifying

dignified washing
splashing ultimate body
deep silent pools
washing reality
no thinking here
attuned washing

without a mirror
forgetting height
girth looks garb
washing my face
wet insight
practicing realizing

my body
not pure impure
body bathes body
moon bathes moon
not washing to get moon
washing clean is moon

bathing body mind
within without
earth heaven
past present future
causes conditions
the whole works clean

woven cloth washing face
willow twig cleaning teeth
wonderful grime grease
washing grime grease
washing life blood
india china japan america

Ode to Eyeballs

ganzei

i whisper praise
to eyeballs seeing clearly
one blink two blinks
eye sight seeing
mountains rivers earth
vitally renewing suns moons

brightness
the real eyeball
the whole dynamic universe
not seeing before after
not preferring
density clarity

eye is sharp
when meeting things
in mutual encounter
two become one
without losing themselves
eye a thunderbolt

already i have
my own eyeballs
yet sometimes i gaze out
as if eyes are elsewhere
this seeking
is eyeballs too

eye begs for itself
eyeballs include
everything everywhere
forgetting inside outside
no sand in eyes
eyes of wonder

gouging out
an old wise one's eyeball
is becoming a person
seeing plum blossoms
in snow fields
the diamond eye

Ode to Mountains Rivers

sansuigyo

i whisper praise
to blue mountains walking
their rhythm my gait
two feet walking
i backward step
into oceans of light

the stone woman
gives birth at night
stone becomes child
child becomes stone
when two mix
each is born

mountain toes
walk on water
free in all directions
mountain sees water
water sees itself
self settles on self

water rises to sky
falling as rivers streams
rushing whirling splashing
stream in a drop
water becoming
a wise person

river is water
mountain is water
water flows
beyond river mountain
beyond form emptiness
no bottling up

once in mountains
no person to meet
waking each day
praising mountains rivers
mountains and wise people
falling in love

Ode to Here Now Mind

soku shin ze butsu

i whisper praise
to here now mind
only budhha always buddha
not brain thinking neurons
not things residing
never certainties

not sitting
a thousand years
even one breath
attaining trying
seeking elsewhere
just here now mind

awakened ones
picking up throwing out
mind weeding
not puffing up
mistaking living
for arriving

mind is fences walls
never wet muddy
open clear present
great inclusion
shapes colors wind sky
precisely this

when mind awakens
heaven falls down
ground tears apart
each thing the whole
the whole each thing
nothing left out

luminous mind
mountains rivers earth
sun moon stars
no adding subtracting
pure bright light
snow falling in moonlight

Ode to Light

komyou

i whisper praise
to luminosity brightness
pure dharma eye
each thing light
self light
universe light

i am lost
when not light
light also lost
standing on feet
holding a friend's hand
both luminosity

east is east
also full compass
home of light
is east
also all directions
listen to brightness

vast light
not blue yellow
red white black gold
beyond ideas
one hundred weeds
utterly clear

going beyond
common sacred
indigo vermillion
of infinite brightness
living dying
light's activity

already i am brightness
not past present future
light gathers itself
becoming each think
now of totality
totality of now

Ode to Truth

doshin

i whisper praise
to truth loving
the luminous moon
the great journey
seeking listening searching
invitations from emptiness

longing for snow
falling in moonlight
a rare calling
some feel deeply
others sleep walk
few circle zen mountain

thoughts slant toward me
body mind an object
forestalling spiritual gravity
when seeing clearly
everything passes
life a slim thread

walking this path
while dreaming awake
i wholeheartedly honor
three treasures
written on my heart
buddha dharma sangha

i sing praise
before during after
now every moment
yes to emptiness
yes to change
yes to everything

i vow to make a buddha
within this lifetime
to fashion out of flowers
incense light snow
silent contemplation
the infinite moon body

Ode to Awakening

genjo koan

i whisper praise
to birds flying
in empty sky
to fish swimming
in endless sea
to all of it

i embrace
body of water bone
body of moon light
old body skin bag
studying self
letting self go

i love flowers
as blooming
as petals on ground
as wild spring weeds
even crowding gardens
always welcome guests

somersaulting in now
frolicking free of myself
water air life
beyond high low
air my breath
water my blood

whether things
be square or round
geometry never confines
fire is fire
ashes are ashes
each the full moon

although freedom
never missing
i practice stillness
breath by breath
commingling things
honing life

Ode to Plum Blossoms

baike

i whisper praise
to plum blossoms in snow
forever buddha's eye
plum blossoms are moonlight
illuminating overhead
illuminating underfoot

plum blossoms
flowers suddenly now
one two three many
each flower always now
spring is flower
flower is spring

plum blossoms
completely wild
unfathomable mystical
flowers wind grass trees
pure intentions
spring fragrance

plum blossoms
all flowers opening
all worlds now
old plum tree
has kindly bequeathed
heaven earth

plum blossoms
buddha here now
turning dharma wheel
eyes completely open
ants grass rain clouds
vital dynamic wondrous

plum blossoms
the boundless expanse
an empty snow field
mind is universe
universe is plum blossoms
inside outside white snow

Warm Zen Practice

A poetic Version of Dogen's Bendowa

Introduction

Dogen's Bendowa encourages sincere and warm hearted Zen practice. Through meditation and dharma study, people can learn to rest in spaciousness and abide in peace and loving kindness. Bendowa is based on the Buddhist philosophy and experience of 'no-self' and the unconditioned reality of existence-being, also called the dharmakaya, the mystical and transcendent body of light.

In order to present the complexities of Bendowa in an understandable and clear way, I eliminated Dogen's redundancies, dogmatism, circularities, anachronisms, Buddhist terms, and dialectical arguments. I also recast his difficult and non-dual philosophical essay into contemporary verses and subdivided the essay into topics with titles.

I hope that by sharing my delight in Dogen's wisdom you might gain some insight into your vast nature.

Body of Light and Space

los viejos old radiant wise people
merged bodies and hearts in blue sky

intuiting all shapes as their own body
they saw light petals raining on everyone

spacious light body an enduring presence
step into it like an old warm coat

walk silently within the rainbow light
already you are buddha of infinite sea mind

leave the sense of 'me' and sky rests in palms
a blessing beyond anything you willfully do

rest peacefully in this essential light home
without gap between you and things

your voice the mysterious rippling
the birth and death of galaxies

slipping inside spaciousness
no words clearly explain it

why divvy up the world like pie
sun and moon are always whole

please return often to sitting in oneness
the cage of self never had bars

An Ancient Longing

search out your heart's desire
that ancient longing for light and space

tossing out fame and fortune
you are the treasured vulnerability

be leery of charmers and pundits
your soft heart can easily be enchanted

sail endless oceans seeking wise people
who can wander like clouds in spaciousness

colored multitudes live as spaciousness
they shower the silent blessing

although marvelously different all enjoy
calm minds focused and wide without goal

do not be lazy respond to the longing
the mystery of subtle spacious presence

you can simultaneously receive and give light
the entire world-cosmos your arms and limbs

what is more fulfilling in this life
than teaching the subtle light body

wait a bit before sharing the radiant light
until the cosmic meal is well digested

once everything is out of your house
teach others to open the windows wide

The Dank Earth is Vastness

no matter what road you travel
spaciousness is everybody's friend

walking into spaciousness
is blessed and blessed again

the dank earth green trees are vastness
beach pebbles granite walls are infinite space

universe-mind the endless big bang
each piece of dust born this precise moment

spaciousness is the great mother
no mental gymnastics can get at it

forget tricks or folderol
to experience yourself as light

let go or your version of life
give up busyness rest in deep silence

ditch 'i'm only my body and mind'
sit still free yourself from concepts

not dividing inner from outer
is the whole sum of existing

feel the exquisite joy and splendor
as your light body breathes vastness

peanut butter fast cars you name it
each great spaciousness outside of concepts

the moment you know yourself as light
all space knows itself as light

the moment you know yourself as light
all things are light and balance

do not underestimate the importance of sitting still
it mystically connects all teachers teachings time

sitting still the denouement of past
precise now the vast luminosity

practicing and resting in calm is intertwined
with incomprehensible vast spaciousness

spaciousness runs through everything you do
sitting still is just one way to know vastness

the sweet world of separateness
already the miraculous spacious unity

so what if your mind and things move about
calm and spacious presence can't be bothered

once you walk as light-spaciousness
enjoy the inside and outside of everything

two rivers flowing in and out of each other

the mystical cooperation of you and all things

after you can walk through myriad light gates
spread the insanity benefit the world-cosmos

In an Ocean of Sky

how sad it is for those
asleep to their vast body

sitting still is not a new fad
it is the essential reality of inter-being

fine words and practices can touch the heart
do not mix these up with calm spacious presence

greed and conceit will drown you
forcing your mind is not peaceful

why doubt such time worn truth
get out of your own way and sit

if you can breathe you can sit
already you are in an ocean of sky

believe in spaciousness
put all you've got into it

take your time and awaken little by little
pay precise attention to now and awaken instantly

when you see as your teacher
you can dwell in joyous spaciousness

the honored cosmic ones
live fully in each spacious moment

An Invitation from Granite Mountains

no school of buddhism is the only right buddhism
the zen flower makes no ridiculous claims

when people of other faiths ask for teachings
we give them warm hearted encouragement

better and worse are one sided misfortune
be wary of people proclaiming high ground

do not get caught in the net
of flowery words and ideas

you need to experience the subtle reality
of spaciousness for yourself

the green earth and granite mountains
invite us into spacious truth

the great vastness is infinitely wide
more abundant than the sum of all things

every atom manifest the arising of truth
the spaciousness of reality

sitting still goes beyond apparent duality
embedded within thoughts feeling concerns awareness

how wondrous to remember that spaciousness
has never been apart from your essential being

the trustworthy zen way relies on wise teachers
confirming students spacious wisdom

Body and Space Entwined

awakening spaciousness is more essential
than precepts equanimity or wisdom

the treasure of spacious inter-being
is the quintessential teaching of buddha

the old worn path of sitting still
dynamic truthful reality beyond compare

do not be misled by names like zen or sitting
the experience of spaciousness has no name

it manifest in standing sitting walking lying
yes wise ones claim sitting the finest gate

when you sit there is nothing to attain
you exist as the original state of spaciousness

everything is included in spacious mind
an even balanced mind holds confusion clarity equally

a beginner sitting still before realization
shares the experience of spaciousness

practice and awakening are not two stages
los viejos the ancient wise ones clarified this

spaciousness always present
sitting matters before and after awakening

when you see the way practice the way
beginners and mature students sit the same

ideas of an eternal mental essence
flies in the face of inter-being

nothing exists separate and apart
no soul nothing immortal nothing eternal

spaciousness and things have always been one
vastness and your body mysteriously entwined

trying to get free of life and death
foolish as thinking a beach pebble is gold

living and dying itself spacious stillness
all reality flashes of lightening this moment

No Second Person

mistake after mistake can not be avoided
continuously benefit from sitting

devotion to sitting still
a sure-fire way to awaken

people of all genders races dispositions
capable of joyful stillness in spaciousness

priests householders salespersons officials murderers
no station precludes awakening

don't let the suffering anguished world
inhibit practicing stillness-spaciousness

you can verify your experience of unity
you know if bath water is warm or cold

the subject object gap won't disappear intellectually
focus your attention and penetrate unity intuitively

sitting in spaciousness is the zen way
before during after intuitive wisdom awakens

anyone awakening stillness-spaciousness
realizes there is no second person

do not depend on external or internal circumstances
keep faith in bright light spaciousness

seeds aplenty of awakened spaciousness are within you
keep maturing in receiving and using them well

be like a wandering cloud without a fixed nature
when exploring the truth of spaciousness

why wait for the right time and place to practice
today is a good day for teaching and learning truth

About the Author

Tai Sheridan, Ph.D., is a poet and Zen priest with forty-three years of training in the Shunryu Suzuki lineage. His poetry transforms ancient Buddhist texts into accessible and inspirational verse. The Buddha in Blue Jeans series presents a modern contemplative approach to spiritual awakening. Tai lives in Marin County, California, where he has raised his four children.

Please visit www.taisheridan.com

to purchase other works by this author.

10714655R00114

Printed in Great Britain
by Amazon.co.uk, Ltd.,
Marston Gate.